The BROKEN PROMISE

RAVI ZACHARIAS

ILLUSTRATED BY LAD ODELL

A Faith Builder Guide can be found on page 32.

Faith Kids is an imprint of
Cook Communications Ministries,
Colorado Springs, Colorado 80918
Cook Communications, Paris, Ontario
Kingsway Communications, Eastbourne, England

THE BROKEN PROMISE
© 2000 by Ravi Zacharias for text and Lad Odell for illustrations

Designed by Pamela Poll Graphic Design
Edited by Kathy Davis

First hardcover printing, 2000
Printed in the United States of America
04 03 02 01 00   5 4 3 2 1

LIBRARY OF CONGRESS CATALOGING-IN-PUBLICATION DATA

Zacharias, Ravi K.
        The broken promise / Ravi Zacharias ; illustrated by Lad Odell.
            p. cm.
        Summary: Anand and his sister Asha agree to exchange their
        collections of marbles and candy, but Anand tries to keep some of his
        marbles and must then ask for forgiveness from both his sister and
Jesus.
        ISBN 0-7814-3451-3
        [1. Christian life—Fiction. 2. Honesty—Fiction. 3. Forgiveness—Fiction.
        4. Brothers and sisters—Fiction] I. Title
        PZ7.Z167 Fo 2000
        [Fic]—dc21   00-022706

This book belongs to:

_____

"Love the Lord your God with all your heart and with
all your soul and with all your mind and with all your strength. . . .
Love your neighbor as yourself.
There is no commandment greater than these."

Mark 12:30-31 (NIV)

There was a man who collected artwork from around the world— beautiful paintings, lovely vases, carved boxes, and other small treasures.

This man and his wife had two children, Anand and Asha. Their names had been specially chosen. Anand means "to be happy," and Asha means "hope."

One day Anand saw his father locking a cabinet full of treasures, and he asked to see inside.

"Of course you may see inside," said his father. "But first you might want to call Asha. She likes to look at the collection too."

The Broken Promise

Life Issue: Learning about God's love and forgiveness
and what it means to love Him fully.

Spiritual Building Block: Integrity/forgiveness

Think About It

Review the story to answer these questions:

- Why did the father collect artwork?
- How did Anand and Asha choose what they would collect?
- What feelings began to cause trouble for Anand?
- How did Anand cheat Asha?
- Why is it important to do what you promise?
- What happens when we are not honest with God?

Talk About It

Share this story with someone else. Talk about your answers to these questions:

- What collections do you have?
- Why are they important to you?
- Have you ever been cheated by someone else? How did you feel? Did you forgive that person?
- Have you ever asked God for forgiveness as Anand did? Was it difficult?
- Why is it good to know that God loves us and forgives us?

Try It

Read the Bible verse on page 3 of this book. Jesus calls this "the greatest commandment of all." Would you like to have a constant reminder of this great commandment? In Jesus' time, God's commands were kept on doorposts so people would see them coming and going. Copy the verse in bright colors and tape it to your bedroom door. Look at it each day, morning and night, until you can say it by heart.

That night before he went to bed, Anand looked at the candy Asha had given him and thought about how good it would taste. But then he remembered something more important. He knelt down and prayed, "Dear Jesus, thank You for what You have taught me. I want You to know that I love You with all my heart. And Jesus, thank You for a sister like Asha who is willing to forgive me."

When he finished, he was happy because he knew how much his family loved him and how much God loved him too. Now he knew that God would always keep His word. Like his name, Anand's heart was filled with joy.

$\mathcal{A}$nand thought seriously about what his dad had said. He realized that not only had he been dishonest with Asha, he had also been dishonest with God, and it had caused him to doubt God's love for him.

Later that day he took Asha the rest of the marbles. "Asha, I did not give you all my marbles, even though you gave me all your candy. I'm sorry." He handed his sister the sock full of marbles and she hugged him.

"I knew you were sorry you gave me the marbles," she said. "I know how much you like them. We can trade back if you like."

Anand thought for a moment. "Maybe I can give you some of the marbles and you can give me some of the candy."

Asha thought this was a good idea. She had enjoyed playing with the marbles, but she really liked her candy too.

After a long silence, Anand admitted, "No, Dad. I hid some of them in my room."

His dad smiled and said, "I'm glad you told me the truth. Now you must apologize to Asha and give her the rest of the marbles."

He continued, "But what makes you think Asha has deceived you? Isn't it because you did not keep your promise to her that you began to doubt Asha's word? You see, Anand, you must think carefully before you make a promise. But then it is important to do what you promised."

"Does God always keep His promises?" Anand asked.

"Of course," his dad replied. "Jesus has promised that if we ask Him to come into our hearts, He does. You will sometimes wonder if Jesus has kept His promise to be with you every moment. That's when you should ask yourself if you love Him with all your heart. You see, if you do not keep your promises to others, you will think they will not keep their promises to you either. So next time you pray, make sure you keep your word to God."

$\mathcal{E}$arly the next morning Anand went downstairs and found his father reading his Bible.

His father knew what was on Anand's mind. "What is the matter, Son?" he asked gently.

"I wonder," said Anand as he sat down, "if Asha gave me all her candy."

"Anand, may I ask if you gave Asha all your marbles?"

$\mathcal{A}$t first the children were both happy. But that night, while Asha quickly fell sound asleep, Anand tossed and turned and could not get to sleep. All night long he kept thinking, *I wonder if Asha gave me all of her candy?*

anything, however, for he wanted to see if Anand would know that what he had done was wrong. At the trading table Asha gave Anand the jar of candy as Anand gave her the jar of marbles.

That afternoon as Anand walked by his parents on his way to exchange his marbles with Asha, his dad could see that the jar did not look as full as it had looked before. His dad did not say

How will I play tomorrow? he wondered. So he decided that maybe he didn't have to give up all his marbles. He took some of his favorites out of the jar and hid them in his room.

Anand scampered back to his room and shut the door. He wanted to look at his marbles one last time. The more he looked at them, though, the more he wondered if he really wanted to give them up.

*H*is mom and dad knew that Anand was not too happy, but decided to wait and see what he would do. They listened as he tried to make a deal with Asha. "I will give you all my marbles if you will give me all your candy," he said.

Asha was surprised, for she knew how much Anand loved to play marbles. Anyway, she was not so sure she wanted to trade.

Anand pulled out some of his shiny new marbles and showed them to her. "You will get a jar of the most beautiful marbles," he said. "You can have so much fun playing with your friends."

Reluctantly, Asha agreed.

She went back to her room and looked at her jar of candy. She still wasn't sure she wanted to give up all her candy, but she had made a deal with Anand and she would keep her word.

Each time he passed Asha's candy jar he would look at it and wish it were all his. He was no longer happy having just marbles.

At first the children were very pleased with their collections. But as time went by, Anand began to wish he had collected candy instead of marbles.

$\mathcal{E}$very Saturday when their father took Asha for a walk to the store, she bought two of each kind of her favorite candy. She would eat one piece and put the other in her candy jar. She liked the lemon drops, for they were both sweet and sour, but her favorites were the strawberry candies. After she ate those she liked to look in the mirror and smile because her tongue and teeth looked all red.

The children began to add to their collections. Each time Anand went to the store, he bought some marbles. Pretty soon his marble jar was full and he had a nice collection of both antique and new marbles. He liked to sit and look at the different colors and patterns. He studied them in the light and spread them around on the floor. He played marbles with his friends every day, and he thought he had the prettiest marbles of all.

Meanwhile, Asha went to the kitchen to talk to her mom. "Anand is going to start collecting marbles," she said. "Maybe I can do the same."

But her mom had a better idea, "Why don't you collect something else—something that you like best."

Asha thought for a while and decided that what she really liked best was candy. "Every time I go to the store I'll buy some extra candy to keep in a jar," she told her mom.

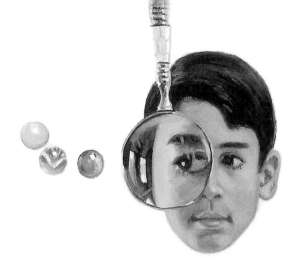

On their way home that evening, Anand said, "I have an idea. I will collect what I like to play with best."

"I know what you're going to say," replied Asha. "You are going to collect marbles."

"You're right," said Anand as he opened the front door. "I already have a nice collection started." He ran to his room to look at his marbles. "Boy, these are pretty," he said as he admired the shining glass balls.

Anand and Asha began to think about what they wanted to collect. The next day, as Asha watched Anand and his friends playing marbles, she thought she might like to collect marbles and play with her friends. The boys dug a small hole in the ground and showed Asha how the game is played.

When Asha joined them, their dad told a story about each piece of artwork and where it had come from. Some of the paintings and silver pieces had been in the family since their grandfather's time; others had been collected by their father.

"Dad, could we collect something valuable like these paintings and vases?" Anand asked.

"Yes, Son, it is good to be a collector of nice things," his father replied. "But a collection does not have to cost a lot of money, you know. It can just be something that helps you keep some happy memories."